# THE PHOENIX SONG

SANGEETA DEB

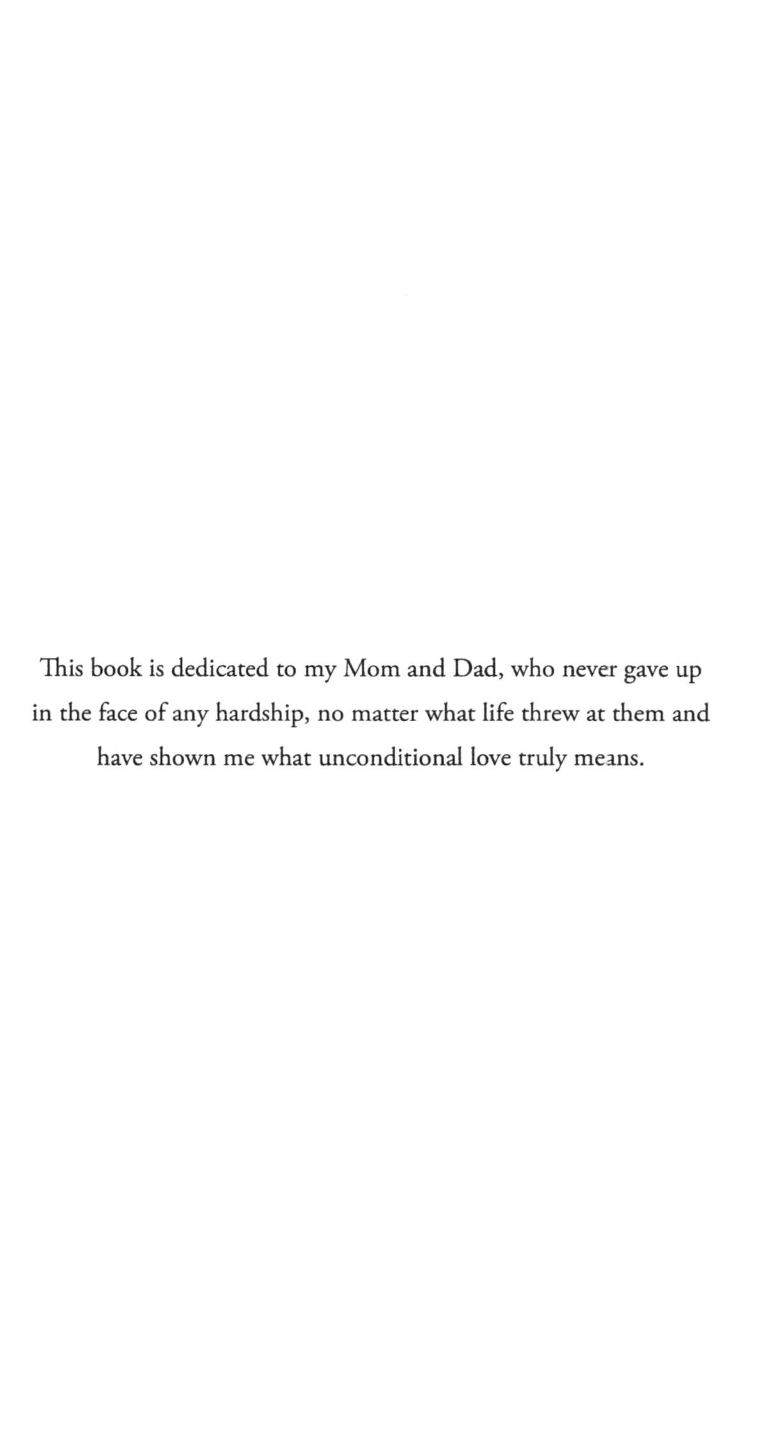

This book is dedicated to my Mom and Dad, who never gave up in the face of any hardship, no matter what life threw at them and have shown me what unconditional love truly means.

# Contents

# Contents

# Acknowledgements

*I am grateful to my best friend, Biswajit, for always being the ray of sunshine- the only constant- in my life when everything else was slipping out of my hands like sand.*

# Prologue

"So you think you know me?" sad Life. "You think you know all the blind turns in my alleys and all the valleys? Haah! What utter folly! Good luck getting to the end of my labyrinth, passing unscathed through the gullies."

# SADNESS

*"I have been travelling for such a long time but I see no end to this road. I have lost so much on the way and I now feel tired and worn."*

# 1. Silence

Silence-
Sometimes silence is deafening,
Sometimes it can't be ignored,
And sometimes it speaks louder than our voices.
Silence-
Sometimes it makes us start screaming,
Sometimes it's all we can afford,
And sometimes it tells the struggle for our choices.
Silence-
Sometimes it lulls us into wistful dreaming,
Sometimes it's a canvas of the losses we scored,
Sometimes it rattles even the most elegant of poises.

# 2. A Child's Plea

I've merely started seeing the world,
My cocoon has just unfurled.
To be able to learn and be able to grow,
Are now the things for me to know.
Now is the time for me to be happy;
To attend school and remain carefree.
Now is the time for me to do some household chores,
But still be free to answer my friends' phone calls.
But now is not the time for me to earn,
Or be traded away for a few bucks in return.
School means homework but it also means fun,
So please don't beat me if the work's not done.
I only trust you- my mom and dad;
So don't let me be petted by people who are bad.
To all other people, I say only this-
I am still a budding flower- don't let me be stamped.

# 3. If Truth be Told

I see you are a trader who trades lives for lies,
And indulges in granting what the wretched desires.
You dare weave a world of deceit,
In the minds of those who are pitifully weak?
You sit in your market all day and connive,
To let the poor souls act on their darkest vice.
You goad people to be jealous and selfish,
To cast aside the need of others and take as they please;
You revel in watching man trade his humanity for a few cents,
And then push him forth until into ruin he descends.
You glorify your heinous deeds in the name of Fate,
And sit proud on your throne and see wars being waged.
So please make haste- don't tarry near me.
Lest I speak out the truth of your lies which I very well see.

# 4. The Same Old Road

As I walk down the same old road,
Every day is a new sight to behold.
Once I saw a few men digging along the roadside,
They seemed to be mending the water pipes.
I saw the road being repaired with pitch one time-
And the air was laden with smoke and grime.
Once I saw a rickshaw-puller,
Haggling with his passenger over the fare.
On the same old road so many cars ply;
But I can't count them all no matter how much I try!
There have been numerous accidents,
On that road these people always tread.
Once I saw an old lady knocked down dead
By a speeding car that afterwards fled.
Two young men doing wheelies on their bikes
Got their ribs broken and lay covered in gore.
And so, as I walk down the same old road,
Every day is a new sight to behold.

# Chapter5

So it's morning and I'm starting again,
Wandering and wondering when I'll find Home.
Where the kitchen had a tile marked by a stain.
Where Dad would stand guard while I
stole some scones.
In that home, Dad would be in his usual chair,
Reading a newspaper and sipping tea.
Disturbing his reading- no one but me ever dared!
'Coz he loved me and would let me be.
Now as I get out of my house for work,
I want to think that I will come back to Home.
Where our lovely maid would put on a smirk,
While doing dishes and slathering foam.
I am in office and lunch time's approaching,
Making me want to go search for Home.
Where Mom would now be done with cooking,
And I'd be eagerly waiting for food on the table.
To know that in the evening, Home would filled-
With the scent of incense and the sound of conch.
Makes me feel that I got a bad hand dealt,
If I can't even find the place where my memories dwelt.
Finally it's night and I'm still wandering,
Trying to search for my fond Home,

Where my Dad would, for me, be waiting,
While listening to the newsreader on TV drone.
But as I enter the house where I now live,
All I see is an empty chair in a room unlit.
And it makes me wish I could find my way back,
To the place that I once called Home and so I sat and wept.

# 6. Time will Heal

The tears that you let fall down,
The fears that you don't speak out loud,
The screams that you lock in and seal,
The anguish that your fists conceal,
The bitterness you restrain,
The scars that paint all your struggles and pain,
Mock the voices that say to you-
"Hush, don't cry, all Time will heal...."

# LOSS OF HOPE

*"There's no hope of finding a way out. I have been searching for the light but only darkness surrounds."*

# 7. Caged

Caged I am, caged in my own mind.
Murderous they are, murderous are my own thoughts.
How they plot, how they scheme
To snuff out my hope and my dreams!
Swirling around, swirling alongside me,
As I cleave and claw at the walls of my mind,
Those thoughts gnaw at me and they scream-
"There's no way out once you are in!"

# 8. The Other Side

I tried to reach for the stars.
But I failed and I fell-
Down, deep down into Tartarus,
Standing before heights I had never scaled.
I gritted my teeth and gathered my strength,
And rallied every cell of my body to obey.
And despite the pain, I managed to crawl out,
Albeit not unscathed and my soul in disarray.
I thought I was strong enough to gather hope once more,
And so I jumped again- this time to reach for the sun.
But it wasn't enough and down I fell again.
Deep down I fell- and found myself in hell.
I knew then that I would never dare,
To reach out for anything for which I cared.
'Coz I didn't know who would answer my call for help,
When even I couldn't do anything for myself.
Then I saw the lone skeletal helmsman figure,
Standing in a boat on the other side of the river,
While all around me, swirled ghastly black figures with soulless eyes,
Whose relentless hungry stares sent shivers down my spine.
I knew then that I was on the wrong side of the river.
And the thought made me seek desperate measure.

So here I am, trying to gather some coins by selling pieces of my soul,
At a penny each to the demons whose gazes I now behold.
And maybe, in my palm if I hold up enough,
Then Charon would take me in his boat, his role reversed,
Back to the other side where the living dwelled,
Where I might yet get to live the life that I knew I deserved.
For which the price to pay is my soul.
And my soul it is, a penny apiece, which to the demons I now sold.

# 9. Darkness Divine

Let's not fear the depths of darkness unfathomed;
Darkness has its own divine rhythm.
Feel that rhythm and groove to it,
And descend into its lowest pit with dancing feet.
Let Darkness protect you with its grace;
When the world burns you like the scorching sun's rays,
Let Darkness take you into its embrace,
And the mockery of the world you need no longer face.
What a strange place the human world is…
It taunts you and pelts you with judgement and jeers,
But it also forces you to conquer your weaknesses and fears,
And when you succeed, it tears you down and drives you to tears.
Because now it is you whom the world fears!
So why be in such a world where cruelty is abound,
When darkness can offer you solace profound?
When darkness takes you under its wings,
Then for the rest of the world you are an obsolete being…

# 10. Vengeance

All the bitterness, all the fear;
All the insecurities, all the envy;
All the hatred, all the despair;
All the hurt, all the rage-
-feel it, acknowledge it,
Take it all in and then let the world see-
See it in your eyes, see it in your walk;
See it in every word you speak,
See it in every deed you do,
See it in every breath you release.
Because you are Fury.
Because you are vengeance.
And you will unleash your avenging grace
On this world that gave it all to you.
'Coz whoever said, "Vengeance is not ours to take"...
...has never had anything taken from them till date.

# 11. One Day I Shall Cry

One day I shall cry for one whole day long,
Shedding tears of acceptance for all that I had forsworn.
I shall let the waters of grief wash away my sins galore,
For losing all that was mine to cherish and mine to hold.
One day I shall lie down smiling and be in peace,
In a meadow full of flowers and brimming with pure bliss.
The memories of my loved ones I shall fondly reminisce,
And I will love Life as it is….
But not today- for today I burn in pain,
Scalding tears of bitter anger, down my cheeks, drain.
My soul torn asunder by thoughts inhumane,
Because today Hell is my only domain.

# 12. Nothing to Lose

So you thought you've hit rock bottom,
By dancing to Fate's mysterious rhythm?
You thought your feet had hit the ground,
Of the dark pit from which you can find no way out?
You thought Fate could not push you any deeper,
Could not push you into darker recesses of this Hell-hole?
Believing there's no more to lose and it cannot get any worse,
You are now giving up on life believing it to be a lost cause?
What dangerous thoughts you have, my silly old friend!
For it is not Fate, but you who scripts your life's journey to the end.
When you failed to fulfil just one dream, you slumped down.
Thinking that there was nothing left to lose, you let yourself drown.
You stopped trying and meekly wore misery's crown.
But while wallowing in self-pity, you even forgot the music you once knew.
Only to realise that you could've done something with that too!
And again you foolishly thought that there would be nothing more to lose,
And again you let yourself fall deeper into despair.
Believing all your efforts would be for naught,

You did not make any effort and touted life to be unfair.
When you lost the people who loved you…
You thought that the last bit of Hope too was taken from you,
And there's nothing more that Fate could pry away from you.
So now here you are, staring into the void with soulless eyes.
Thinking that you're irreparably broken.
That you're nothing but an empty husk-
Dreams and wishes long forgotten.
You think you are a hapless, hopeless living dead,
Destined to be a prisoner in cruel Fate's hand?
Well don't be duped by Fate into believing that it cannot get any worse!
You might think that there's nothing remaining in Life for you,
You might think that you are standing on hard ground under you,
But then you will start falling again as Life takes it course…
And you will realise that there will always be greater, darker depths,
Waiting for you to fall into and even more dearer things to lose.
No matter how much you suffer and how much you lose,
There will always be something more to cherish and something more to lose.
Because you are breathing, because you are feeling,
Because you are human and this is your Life,
So there will always remain something more for you to lose…

# FORGIVENESS AND PEACE

*"I have cried and I have lost. I have fought and I have conquered. I have been burnt and hurt a lot. But making them a bitter memory cost me my soul. So I let go- let go of all the pain and all the sadness that i had in me stored. And I found peace and believe me that it cost me naught."*

# 13. When Truth is a Lie

Will you listen to only sweet words?
There's a lot to learn and lot to know.
But if you refuse to listen,
Then your life's a no-show!
While a lie is an easy-to-believe sweet concoction,
The truth might either be pleasant or be nasty.
But to seek out peace and weed out deception,
The truth needs to be accepted with grit and honesty.
Truth is peace;
Truth is redemption.
And if you can own it,
Then it is your salvation.
So every time you want to hide,
Don't forget to remember that,
Only to the selfish mind,
An inconvenient truth is nothing but a lie!

# 14. The Language You Need Not Speak

Languages spoken in this world are many.
But to be heard without speaking is a wish on every penny.
If speaking your mind doesn't open the door,
Why not see if silence works more?
The silence of the jungle purveys the fear,
When a predator on the hunt is coming near.
Hidden and resolute, as the sniper sets up his rifle,
It is his silence that speaks and not his shuffle.
Silence conveys the sorrow of your heart,
When you mourn the death of the person you loved.
But a person who can't speak and wishes to be heard,
Isn't their silence the loudest amongst all?
Let us not ignore the language of silence;
Or shove those away who use it in their defense.
Because sometimes when you can't utter a word,
You silence cocoons you and screams out to the world.

# 15. Rejoice

I have seen the world,
And I have seen myself too.
I know the nature of Man,
And I know mine too.
I have seen the sufferings of others,
And I have suffered too.
I have faced the mockery of society,
And I have mocked too.
I have seen the joy in people's lives,
And I have been joyous too.
I have seen the tears on some poor soul's cheeks,
And I have shed tears too.
And so I rejoice!
'Cause I know that I am enough…
Enough- not just for myself.
But for the whole world too.

# 16. Shadow and Light

Walking in the darkness of shadows,
I see the shining light too,
And also the greys that remain in between.
And so peace is pervasive;
It slips in through.
The peacock has its flamboyance,
And colours up the day, being a lively sprite.
But the nightingales are waiting,
And the mockingbirds too!
To sing to me in the mellow moonlight.
That which is bathed in the bright daylight,
Cannot always be the only right.
The darkness shrouding the night,
And that twining around our minds,
All lay to rest in the erring human heart.

# 17. Under the Deodars

Walking under the Deodars that take up the sky,
I look up at them and then I realise,
How enchanting and majestic they seem to be,
With sunrays streaming through their canopy!
And I can only look up and stare,
As their greatness strips me bare.
They rise up and up, standing proud and tall,
Like the ancient Greek gods of Olympus' Hall.
An insignificant being- that's all that I am,
Being amongst these giants and so, still I stand.
And spellbound I am, spellbound that I am,
Being amidst them and yet underneath, so still I stand.

# 18. A Good Place

Today I am in a good place,
And am in no haste.
No more running in the rat race,
And no more faith misplaced.
Everything that I see,
I see simply with my own eyes.
No more sowing doubts' seeds,
And no more reaping spies.
No more questioning my own ability,
And no more caring for others' gaze.
I do what gives my soul stability,
Opinions of others? Nah…I'm unfazed.

# LIGHT AT THE END OF THE TUNNEL

*"I have come a long way . When I thought that all was lost, I still did not stop. I carried on and held on to hope. Finally I stand- at the end of the tunnel. And what a sight it is to behold- light welcoming me back once more!"*

# 19. Teacher

I was so small,
And I was so scared;
The first day that my mother held my hand
And into school she led.
Tears rolled down my chubby cheeks,
As I struggled with my mother
To get my hand freed.
But then you smiled at me,
Dear Teacher of mine!
Who wiped my tears and took my hand.
You made me learn the Alphabet,
And taught me how to add and subtract.
You taught me how to draw and colour.
And you looked so happy,
When I gave you a flower.
But you were so angry,
When your lessons I didn't pay heed to.
And yet it is you, O dear Teacher,
Whom I shall always admire and look up to.

# 20. Today's Canvas

It's the morning of a new day,
Waiting for us to paint our way.
Let's see what we have with us,
To make the frame and form the canvas.
Then we shall decide the palette,
For what we want to paint and create.
Now we choose the four bars-
-of job, family, food and fame.
And join them together,
To make today's frame.
But to make it square…
…duh, that would be pretty lame.
Hmm…for today, let's increase the bar of job,
And shorten that of fame.
Or might it be good to change the bar of family and food,
And let the rest remain?
Now that we have made a frame of our choice…
Let's pick some colours to make the palette joyous!
So many different colours of life to choose from!
Which of these might get added,
To have today's canvas adorned?
Ah, look, with hope the canvas is already gessoed!
Soon hurdles and disappointments will sand it.

And once it's toughened, then we can paint it.
For today's palette, let's settle with-
-love and determination, perseverance and grit.
Let's also put a dollop of empathy,
To make the palette look really pretty.
Let the brushes for today be our thoughts and hard work.
To grace the canvas with strokes quick or broad!
As each brush dips into a new life colour,
And flies across the canvas to the border,
It fills up the space with happiness and grief.
Each stroke lights up a spot with life,
Each stroke turns the canvas into success or strife,
Showing us the colours in which we believe.
As time passes by, the canvas gets filled.
Replete with the colours of life, it is brightly stained.
And here we are at the end of the day-
Standing and admiring our work of today.
So many colours still left to use.
So many canvases still left to fill.
So let's wake up tomorrow to another day.
And begin afresh to paint life's way.

# 21. The Flickering Streetlight

Who says I want to be the burning sun's light?
That, upon all, I want to shine equally bright?
I say I want to be that flickering streetlight,
The one that suddenly flares to life,
Just as some tired old soul passes by.
I want to be that one moment for some poor guy,
When they can say to themselves with a quite sigh-
"Yes! Finally something for me went right!"

# 22. Ephemeral

Lying down on the ground,
And looking up at the sky,
Finding animals, birds and whatnot!
In the fluffy white clouds as they fly by.
Walking on the soft green grass,
Finding dandelions heralding spring;
Blowing on the puffballs to make them scatter,
And see them being whisked away like snowflakes by the wind.
With a book in one hand, coffee in the other…
Sitting beside the window during the monsoon rains.
Watching the rain droplets pattering on the glass,
Making tiny rivulets as they run down the panes.
Welcoming winter during the early mornings,
Amongst the reeds and the taro leaves;
Where one flick of the hand
Makes the dew drops slip!
Ephemeral are they all.
And ephemeral are all things of beauty…
…and so is this Life,
That only once we get to live.

# 23. You Are Beautiful

You know that you will sneeze,
If you breathe the pollen in the breeze.
Yet you bow down to admire the flower,
That is blooming in the bower.
And so you are beautiful.
You know that you might get bitten,
If you help the dog that had its leg broken.
Yet you get down on your knees,
To tend to the animal's injuries.
And so you are beautiful.
You know that you might be scolded,
If you reach home late though unintended.
Yet you pull down the kite that's stuck in a tree,
To give it back to the child who's on a crying spree.
And so you are beautiful.
When your thoughts are kind and your deeds kinder,
When your eyes see every creature,
With impartial love and pure wonder,
Then you're every bit as beautiful,
As your mother wanted you to be at the time of her Labour.

# 24. Hope

I am the Elixir of your Life.
I fuel your dreams and nourish your thoughts.
I sweep away your fear of all things foul,
And urge you forth to reach your goal.
I am a soothing touch to your turbulent mind.
I am the ever-glowing flame that warms your life.
I am the Phoenix rising from the ashes of your failure.
I am the hand that you hold when you are unsure.
I guide you through the swamps of life's struggles,
And give you strength to break your shackles.
I make you march through storms of hail,
And keep you focused on your aim.
I always fight against despair,
And I am known to be Moros' bane.
Don't let go of me ever!
Because I am the spirit of Elpis-
who never left Pandora's Jar.
Because I am the Elixir of your Life…
Because I am…Hope.

# 24. I

I am

I feel

And

I don't

Because I

Becau

# REDEEMING GLORY

*" The faith in myself is all I need to know that one day I shall very well succeed. Knowing the worth of all the time and effort I spent is the path towards glory and I shall be redeemed."*

# 25. Treat Them Light

You don't wanna try;
But you cannot deny,
That whatever made you cry,
Has to be bid goodbye.
The reasons for your tears,
Are what your mind fears.
But, if to beat 'em is what your heart desires.
Then let that desire stoke your soul's fire.
Wallowing in self-pity and drowning in misery-
May come to us pretty fast and easy.
But treat them light and keep your mind breezy.
And you will be freed from their grip in a jiffy.

# 26. Conquer

They entered the concrete jungle,
Hoping to conquer.
They would overcome every hurdle-
Of this, they were sure.
They dreamt of making it big,
With their strange ideas.
And thought that they could succeed,
Shedding conventional criterions.
But then they saw the long queue,
And got to understand the "right channel".
They came to know about favours due,
And they concluded their morals to be banal.
So they ditched their bag of ideas,
And got onto the road homeward bound.
But the further they got away from their goal,
The more they wanted to turn around.
'Coz who wants to give up so easily, right?
If you have a dream,
You need to hold onto it tight,
Till every cell in your body chants it the same.
And so they did- they did turn around,
With renewed fervour they began afresh.
Believing only in hard work and knowledge profound,

They refused to be any longer digressed.
The queue then parted, it did part for them
Because they were a force of their own;
They were the pioneers who always stood firm,
From a challenge, they never backed down.

# 27. Reborn

To be someone's pet project,
To be someone's charity case,
To be a human piece that has defect,
To be a memory that's easy to erase.

To be a pawn in someone's mind games,
To be the one pushed from here to there,
To be a face absent from all picture frames,
To be a puppet to whom everybody is a puppeteer-

'Tis okay if you haven't gone through all that.
But it is okay even if you have.
It is indeed an existence to be scoffed at.
And an existence from which you need to save yourself.

So when you are told that you are an eyesore,
When you think you can't break this vicious cycle anymore,
Close your eyes and reach out to your own soul.
Shake off the grime,push your hardest and you shall soar.

Unfurling your wings might seem a hassle.
But when you pity yourself no more,
Mockery by others will no longer be your shackle.

You will fly and winds of freedom,under your wings, shall roar.

# 28. You Are Mine

Where is the hum of your heart?
Or have you felt the tingle from a touch?
Where's the light that was once in your eyes?
Where's the thirst for life,
That you once promised to yourself you won't deny?
You want to find your moment?
Do you really do?
Then where is the madness,
That, in your mind, used to brew?
You want to be the happiness in others' lives?
But without finding that of your own,
How will you survive?
Do you know what you want to make thine?
Then reach out and grab it,
Earn it or take it,
And say, "You are mine!"

# 29. Celebration

I AM...
A reason to smile,
A lesson to be learnt,
A promise to be kept,
A goal to be reached,
A mystery to be solved,
A path to be discovered,
A journey to be completed,
A success to be congratulated,
A ray of sunlight to be felt.
All that and yet I am also
A failure to be remembered,
A veil of darkness to be ripped,
A death to be mourned;
I am Life-I am always the beginning,
My end a new beginning too.
Celebrate me all the time;
For nothing in this world has shades as varied as mine.

# 30. The Phoenix Song

Am I floating or walking, dreaming or awake?
I know not and nor can I tell.
For I am veiled in darkness as I move ahead.
With silence announcing my every footstep.
I know not what I left behind.
I know not what I will find in front.
But there ain't no thing called a tragic past,
And there ain't no thing called an unseen future.
What I have is what I had,
Taken in, absorbed and into my soul fed.
Disappointment and betrayal? I've had quite a few.
Hurdles and failures? Duh! Had 'em too.
And with all that in me, I still march on.
Until the darkness ebbs and I see the sun.
And under that sun, I burst into flames, bright and tall.
Because this is my Phoenix Song and now…I am reborn.

How you let your mind perceive the value of your life is how you shall live it.

Printed by Libri Plureos GmbH in Hamburg,
Germany